The Optimist

The Optimist

Joshua Mehigan

OHIO UNIVERSITY PRESS

ATHENS

Ohio University Press, Athens, Ohio 45701
www.ohio.edu/oupress
© 2004 by Joshua Mehigan

12 11 10 09 08 07 06 05 04   5 4 3 2 1

Library of Congress Cataloging-in-Publication Data
Mehigan, Joshua, 1969–
   The optimist : poems / Joshua Mehigan.
      p. cm.
   ISBN 0-8214-1611-1 (cloth : alk. paper) — ISBN 0-8214-1612-X (pbk. : alk. paper)
   I. Title.
   PS3613.E425O68 2005
   811'.6—dc22

                                        2004017143

Acknowledgments

The author gratefully acknowledges the following journals, in which some of these poems first appeared: *The Carolina Quarterly* ("A Broken Home"); *The Chattahoochee Review* ("After a Nightmare," "An Ideal Passion," "'If Ye Find My Beloved . . . ,'" "A Questionable Mother," "Runaway Daughter"); *Cimarron Review* ("The Pig Roast," "Two New Fish"); *Cumberland Poetry Review* ("Déjà Vu," "The Spectacle"); *Dogwood* ("Promenade," "The Umbrella Man"); *The Formalist* ("The House Swap," "Last Chance at Reconciliation," "The Tyrant"); *Hellas* ("The Swan Song"); *Illinois Review* ("A Bird at the Leather Mill," "The Birthday Gift," "A Lot of Noise," "The Suicide"); *Orbis* ("The Murder"); *Pivot* ("The Festival"); *Ploughshares* ("Confusing Weather," "The Mayor"); *Poetry* ("The Optimist"); *The Sewanee Review* ("The Abject Bed," "Buzzards," "A Contract"); *Unsaid* ("After Last Call," "Family Gathering," "Past Bedtime," "Retirement"); *Verse* ("The Story of the Week"); *Wind Magazine* ("Progress").

For William and Lisa Mehigan,
and for Betty Smith

His voice broke when he spoke the magic word.
The rag tossed up did not become a bird.

Contents

II

I

Promenade

Bowne Park, Queens. Labor Day morning. A man stumbles across a wedding.

This is the brief departure from the norm
that celebrates the norm. The wind is warm
and constant through the field set at the heart
of the impervious borough, yet apart.
This day and this place, born from other days
and places as a parenthetic phrase,
and this sky, where a businessman may write
the purposeless, brief beauty of a kite,
are like the possibilities of love.
The kite leaps up, rasps fifty feet above
until it is almost unusual,
and fastens there. The wind's predictable
but private method with it sets it free
to dive toward greater plausibility
and finish its digression in the wide
municipal burlesque of countryside.
What distantly appear to be festoons
of white, white bunting, trefoils of balloons
in white, improve the black affectless trees
where three girls stand like caryatides
patiently holding crepe bells to a bough.
Something exceptional will happen now.
But first the fat, black, windswept frock will swerve
past the buffet to steal one more hors d'oeuvre.
He floats like an umbrella back to where
his book is, smoothes his robe, and smoothes his hair.

Yellow grass undulates beneath the breeze.
Couples file through the corridor of trees
toward rows of folding seats. Bridesmaids unhook
from groomsmen's arms. Every face turns to look;
and when the bride's tall orange bun's unpinned
by ordinary, inconvenient wind,
all, in the breath it takes a yard of hair
to blaze like lighted aerosol, would swear
there was no greater miracle in Queens.
Wish is the word that sounds like what wind means.

Two New Fish

Inside the knotted plastic bag he tossed
and caught in front of him the whole way home
were two new fish. They seemed to him to bear
a trademark not quite rare, as though the two
were penknife souvenirs from the next county.
The fish were alien and mediocre.

He felt his strength as if it were a bomb
that detonates with no complexity
of wires or clocks, fuse or even impact.
His tosses changed without much thought to heaves.
They arced, slowed, hung like miniature flames
trapped in a bubble, glanced the power lines . . .

The fish sped back an inch and forth an inch
in the bag cupped in the boy's hands, and then
not in his hands at all, then on the grass.
He rolled the bag experimentally
over the gravel drive to demonstrate
again how well he kept from breaking it.

He hung it on a stick and jabbed the air
fitfully, like a hobo shooing bees.
He did his undecided best to burst
and also not to burst the bag. And when
within these limits neither fish had died,
the boy put down the bag and went inside.

A Questionable Mother

The camera crews were gone home for the evening,
an infant dead, but then again, as always,
the white globes fading on above the entrance.
The estranged boyfriend stayed with family, resting.
The suspect's parents clasped hands in the foyer.
Their daughter was once more a daughter only,
yet, blood or no, unsound or no, no daughter.
Not calm but quiet settled in the station,
in all who'd heard her cry they must believe her.
The suspect's father petted a police dog,
and felt, without remarking, it was pregnant.
The cracked, hard leather chairs were now familiar.
Life's fell astonishments were now familiar.
Here thoughts of murder weren't all that uncommon.
Nakedness was uncovered by the hour.
Within, the suspect cried they must believe her.
The female officer behind a window
of thick green glass typed slowly without stopping.
Beneath the squat cap holding in her hairdo,
her face suggested she withheld her judgment.
The unleashed shepherd lay beside her, licking.
She didn't look at it, but typed on, thinking
animals always know when they are dirty.

The House Swap

That night the town was far behind somewhere,
and now the city lay there in the road,
a velvet box, ribboned with braids of light.
They slept in an apartment where the view
of quiet boats remanded them to sleep
but wakened them in time to go, to do.

The first day was a famous monument
they spotted from afar but never found.
The second put them in a drowsy bar
where afternoon became a narrow sound
of traffic sloshing through the rainy day.

The next few days were duty. What they saw
were underneaths of bridges, lines at doors.
Their nights were the apartment, where the view
at dusk was gull-swarmed barges hauling junk.

Meanwhile, the ones they swapped with sat and learned
what country life is like, upon a porch.
The husband, from the window, watched the storm.
His aging wife, in bed, no longer called.

The storm arrived as though on time somewhere,
the blue tarp on the woodpile lifting up,
blowing and floating higher in the gray,
until by dusk it seemed a woman's gown
that never floated, as he'd hoped, away.

The Umbrella Man

He looks well past the people briskly passing,
those morning faces patient for a springtime,
peering out at his pushcart from beneath
their black or scarlet, lilac or transparent,
their bitterly ironic polka-dotted—
some nearly shredded from their fragile frameworks,
some neat as arctic tents, grotesquely hale—
their sundry, jostling, myriad umbrellas.
Steadfastly, though the rush-hour crowd starts thinning,
he stares into this morning so like evening
because he seeks the one he knows will come:
one always just about to turn the corner,
blushing, and misty-faced, and misty-haired,
skirting the storefronts, beautifully bereft,
who has left home this morning unprepared.

The Spectacle

The fire transformed the bedspread into fire.
It climbed the curtain like a nervous cat,
and at the top it rained onto the floor,
where vapor reeked from cracks between the boards.
They slept a moment more but didn't wake
until the gas was on them like a tongue,
and then they were asleep again. The fire
waited behind the front door like a person
of great importance just about to step
onstage. The town stood back a bit and watched
as colors in the window changed from clear
to black to orange; as the smaller panes
plunked out onto the porch; and then because
the firemen said, "Stand back, please . . . please stand back . . ."

An Ideal Passion

Even at home
he was as inward as the limbless tree
that leaned above the plaster gnome,
the tree the birds seemed not to see.
But he intended nothing else.

Then at his job he saw a girl
as outward as the curling roots
that quietly broke his cellar wall.
On Thursday night he paced the hall,
wondering what it was that made him curl.

At work, the work went on. Meanwhile, she
went this way, pretty, past his chair
and that way leaned against a door
and smiled or nodded at him and others there,
intending nothing, thinking nothing more.

Each night, he pictured her above his bed
like sparks collected in the air above
a fire that burns for one late, sleepless eye.
Then, in the quiet, he could hear the sound
of love already curling up to die.

A Bird at the Leather Mill

The crane stood in the center of the floor
of the mill, lost and tentative. Its bill
looked like a fancy awl with a down handle.
It wore its wings as though they were a shawl
thrown on an idiot. At first the men
imagined that a person had strolled in
like a green salesman or a debutant.
And when the crane walked toward the loading dock,
the men on tiptoe prowled with laundry bags
to grab and hold it like a secret hope
harbored in exile. Later on, at lunch,
they took turns, each explaining what he'd do
if it came back. They bragged, or chaffed, aware
the thing was lost, but never saying so.

In the Home of My Sitter

Mrs. Duane Krauss, sure of her solitude,
grimaced between the kitchen alcove's cryptic
lesser motifs of Elvis and Saint Jude,
herself the central subject of the triptych:
her young-old country cheeks and looming bust,
the timely smile, gathered around a lie.
She called me "dear," she bowed, she briefly fussed,
then turned to pat her mother's china dry.

I did my part. I showed how bright I was,
how self-assured. But I lacked common sense.
Even the dogs there knew—and not because
she humbled them with cozy sentiments—
that friends, not being family, not quite,
keep out of trouble and keep out of sight.

    • • •

Across the white hill swallows fanned and scattered,
drawing my eye along till I could see
atop the hill—tilted and mossy, flattered
by early sun—an old barn, tempting me.
Morning to suppertime not much else mattered.
They must've known. I wanted them to know.
Morning to suppertime their still den chattered
with *Meet the Press* and Christian radio.

Patient, I watched the barn's roof simplify
to silhouette, and the hillside's azure glow

pass, as the night retuned my errant eye,
to static white, the white of moonlit snow,
while those four faces I've not seen again
kept to the borrowed twilight of the den.

. . .

One face there, bright as ripening persimmon,
still a bit bitter, seldom looked at me:
that quiet *Vater* stooped amid his women,
who let his lenses flash for privacy.
High in the shadow of a naked rafter,
his stuffed barn owl outspread its furious wings,
a household daemon to discourage laughter,
unnecessary talk, and touching things.

. . .

Mother, my young, my beautiful rescuer!—
so late, so long, I might be waiting still,
my pure heart wondering always where you were,
if not for those four strangers on their hill,
who, loath to form a fair impression of me,
simply did not, as you must always, love me.

Déjà Vu

Autumn debris was laid out on the walk
like a garish rug. The trees weren't merely red.
But paper leaves adorned the blackboard's edge
with red alone, as if the whole fall scene
were judged to be some treacherous romance.
Behind the door, a woman stood and smiled
toward the low, wooden cubbyholes for coats.
The mothers' lipsticked mouths persuaded new
miniature suits and dresses to sit still
on the gray rug, beneath the flag, beside
the piano. Teacher played a tune and sang.
The children cried, or sang. The mothers left.
The new girl hid beneath the desk till noon.

But now it isn't autumn. Winter's here.
Now Teacher has been buried thirty years,
the decades spent like afternoons at home.
White paper snowflakes pinned to robes bear names
outdated as the names of cars they rode in —
Packard, or Hudson — traded in for chairs
with wheels their hands are not advised to try.
The one who hid beneath the desk rolls in,
the new girl one last time, in a gown that is
only white, as the snow is only white.
She stares at rows of faces that transmit
nothing: Here is the piano but no song.
Her daughter's lipsticked mouth says something . . . What?
The nurse is bringing blankets. Winter's long.

Past Bedtime

A child five years old

A sip of wine. Then the tall chef
behind a climbing fire,
nodding So long, So long,
and the walk to the car.
There, trees and high grasses,
the wind combing them
with a noise like water flooding
a distant reservoir.
Hands large beneath his arms.
The ragtop's canvas odor.
The dark of the jump seat,
the hum through the little carpeted shelf
of the just-sparked motor.
And, up front, murmurous voices,
familiar as himself,
and the blue light,
the blue hand changing gear
through the damp of the dark hills,
through the first fallen leaves,
like cut tobacco or molasses
thickening the air.
Then nothing till the turn,
the lurch up the drive,
sound arms, and slow rousing
on the topmost stair.

The Tyrant

When he came in before his wife, as always,
and hung his jacket on the hook, and sat,
and noted for the thousandth time the dull ways
that beams streamed through the panes and crawled the floor,
he recognized for once the light that strained
toward him. It was mercy. And the more
he tried to see it as a passing phase,
the more his marriage seemed to be just that:
a casual failure, not worth blame or praise,
but tolerance. Outside, it gently rained —
a sun shower, something odd, an easy clue
that life's not merciless, but scatterbrained.
A rainbow circumscribed the joy he feigned
as the key turned; as she ducked past, withdrew.

After Last Call

They tossed up their hands. Home wasn't calling them.
Home, they all cried, is not where you hang your hat.
Home is where you hang yourself, they said,
eyeing the light as wan as tomorrow.
The street was barren. The moon and low sun
ogled each other over the storefronts'
soaped white windows and darkened doors,
as for them alone a quarter mile
of stoplights clicked from red to green.
Diner, a sign said. The sign meant either
quick repartee with a damp-browed young waitress
and the cheapest breakfasts they could think of, or
arch repartee with a sour waitress
and the cheapest breakfasts they could think of.
Diner, the sign said. And so they were diners.
Smoothing their fronts and climbing stone steps, they found
sad yellowed walls, fluorescent lighting,
pancakes, blank faces, a toilet—found home.

Riddle

I'm not a convict,   but sentries stand by,
reluctant to let me   leave my post.
Alone at length,   I leewardly wander,
but few times farther   than a few inches
as the wind whiffs   through my wide-open mouth.
Neither sinning myself   nor slack at my duties
(of which there is one   and one only),
it's capital   that I kill without mercy.
My motive's not mine,   my method impartial,
and, tough as I am,   one tug's my undoing.
Spare yourself   suspense and grief:
Don't do as I do,   but do as I say,
whether sure what I am   or sure what not.

Imperative of the Minor Florentine Chapel

For Shoshanna Wingate

The dusty light here, harsh and dignified,
has somehow brushed each ritual ornament
with its most likely glory, somehow pried
an essence from each stiff expedient.
The light that rings the cross's injured brass
lets me, and the mystic furniture, alone,
leaving sufficient shade for sun to pass
minutely through the yellow stained-glass throne
and, after its long odyssey, alight
on some great passage in the crumbling book.
What other artist has this power or right?
Just hope: to apprehend it with a look,
to feel that something like it could be mine—
know that what drew me here is not divine.

Another Pygmalion

Metropolitan Museum of Art. Standing before Balthasar van der Ast's Flowers in a Vase with Shells and Insects, the painter awaits his friend.

A salamander, a ceramic jar
hatched blue with mandarin birds, a pink half brain,
a mad canary. What are these? These are
(my top lens shows me) nothing less mundane
than tulip, iris, rose, and yellow rose.
Vehement, yes, but otherwise quite sane,
quite natural, in fact, if we suppose
that flowers possess their own fey inner lights.
The iris weighs its bracing indigos
against the ordered ardor that ignites
below, and, though a few stems stand too high,
it alone rises to outlandish heights
over the sullen vessel to defy
all laws of aerostatics, and thus art
must bear the burden of a butterfly-
of-stone's alighting . . . One can't be too smart
when Nature is at stake! One must assume
God's mind, man's spirit, and a serpent's heart,
come clean if one year's rental of a room
costs less than one flamed tulip, and record
the truth about which weeks what flowers bloom,
lest all we never knew and can't afford
be varnished over, bought up, hung, ignored.

Or maybe what my young friend says is true.
That brat should be here! "'Attaboy, Teach—still

stickin' it to The Man at sixty-two."
Cruel, cruel! Perhaps she'd choose some imbecile
with dreadlocks and a sketchbook to uphold
her pretty judgments, with an espadrille
kick me when I said something dry and cold
to our new friend; and then the prim routine
of sudden seriousness, as she extolled
the joy of red, some curve she found pristine,
or patronized me with the details set
in Beauty's outskirts: touchy bee, drab green
grasshopper, hidden thorns; or better yet
the gnarled old spider; and, for last rites, those
three petals on the slab. Next comes regret.
Why I put up with this God only knows.
But how wise youth is! You, too, must be wise,
flamed tulip, iris, rose, and yellow rose,
whose grace a single thought could brutalize.
Being too quick for thought, it never dies.

The Swan Song

The retired actor watched the sky grow dim.
The porch, walled in by junipers and stone,
seemed a setting, a set, for someone else,
though it was his alone.

He leaned along the wall as he once had
at restaurant bars to eavesdrop on the chatter,
though here the alders asked continually
the same thing: "What's the matter?"

But then, sometimes, gravel against a tire,
or the blown page of a book left on his chair,
or ice that settled in a forlorn glass
applauded his despair.

Those times he'd step inside the sliding door,
enchanted with his high, tragic style,
pull down the curtains on the maudlin moon,
and crack his old, arch smile.

The Murder

The man could tell this story by himself,
only love moved him past the terminus of voice.

He'd made a language out of adoration,
but then his mouth was too much dulling eloquence.

And then she left him sitting in a chair,
where his dumb fists fell in his lap like poisoned birds.

His choice became to die, or else to die.
His lack of choice became his life, and language left him.

But he had gestures just as good as words,
and when he spoke again, he spoke with those. They said,

"The way to a woman's heart is through her chest."

Progress

On that Friday, his hands felt to him
as light as though they were nothing, while
in truth nothing was in him, around him,
substantial, pervasive, and all of that—
even atomic: Nothing sat in the drive,
not blocking his way, always letting him look
far into the backyard, never dulling its green,
conceding the smoke its prerogative passage
straight up the flue and out. He felt
that nothing could prevent him then.
The world could never have kept him out,
for he had so little opposition,
had a lack of important opposition,
as the utter darkness is a lack of white light,
and a look from his eyes that could one day have blistered
the paint off a house like nothing.
By Sunday night he found himself
cursing the way a penny fell.

Post Partum

"...its hour come round at last..."

To change now or go underground is vain.
The grasping hands that touch your cheek with snot
soon feed the monster's mouth, to whom it's plain
what you should once have strangled you could not.
It stands there at the door and screams instead.
You knew, once, who you were; but soon you'll see
that you must fall down at its feet as dead,
craving the days you craved humility.
Then one day you will find it's gone away.
Some part of you must turn up missing too.
But these times pass. Some day, though not that day,
you'll wonder if it ever thinks of you;
and, fumbling for just what it was you felt,
you too will mock the ground where once you knelt.

War Dims Hopes for Peace

Nothing Will Be the Same in Land of Free
    Around the World, a Call for Faith and Prayers
Job One Must Be Return to Normalcy
    Bin Laden Praises God as World Despairs

Muslins Report Slurs, Threats, Obscenities
    Hundreds of Bomb Threats, Hoaxes Follow Violence
Bad News for US Civil Liberties
    Madonna Fans Observe a Moment's Silence

"All Necessary and Appropriate Force"
    More Rescue Workers Hurt as Search Turns Damp
Flight Schools Performed No Background Checks, Says Source
    It's Safety First as Yankees Open Camp

Frasier Creator Was "Kind, Classy Man"
    One Hundred Ninety Dead at Pentagon
Evacuations in Afghanistan
    And, Valiantly, the Gruesome Work Goes On . . .

"If Ye Find My Beloved..."

He shut the book. A gentle pebble-crack
against the window stirred him from his bed.
He touched his wife's stiff arm and eyed her back
the way a child confronts an almanac.
There was time left for something to be said
as his shape broke the lamplight crescented
in the dark hall and his boots once again
thudded across the porch. She slept instead.
She didn't hear the music or the men,
the fan belt clucking like a worried hen
out of the driveway, up the road, to where
the bars erased a day's work for a ten
and change. Nor did she quite *not* hear. Out there,
between a half-dreamt porch and headlight glare,
love lowered its muzzled head, growled in defeat,
and dragged its chain across the bottom stair.
Meanwhile, in town, he had his bourbon neat,
told lies, hurled darts, watched skirts float down the street
until all passed and, passing fast, blew out
the small, blue pilot light of his deceit.
The car wove home. Soon day broke like a shout
and stirred black birds from every field. No doubt
it stirred her too. So be it. He was back,
little to tell, and less to talk about.

The Optimist

The film showed stars of varying magnitude,
the left side Libra, and the right side Cancer,
mapping the brain's horizons, vanishing points
respectively of reason and desire.
The doctors liked her cheerful attitude,
hope being all she had in her position.

She waited, calm. Touch burned out first, then vision.
Emotion slipped. Last would be lungs and heart.
But, noting trends, they told her taste was next.
She asked then, could they pick out her last dress?

She wasn't making light. It seemed to her
that cancer just rehearsed life's attitude
that one's desires must taper to a point,
which has position, but no magnitude.

Confusing Weather

.

The sun came to in late December. Spring
seemed just the thing that flattered into bloom
the murdered shrubs along the splintered fence.
The awnings sagged with puddles. Roads were streams.
Wet leaves in sheets streaked everything with rust.
The man who raked his lawn transferred a toad
too small to be a toad back to the woodpile.
In the countryside, he thought he spied the trust
that perished from his day-to-day relations.

His head was like a shoe box of old pictures,
each showing in the background, by some fluke,
its own catastrophe: divorce, lost friends,
a son whose number he could not recall—
this weather, nothing but a second fall,
ending, if somewhat late, just how fall ends.
Each day that week he sat outside awhile
and watched his shadow stretch and disappear.
Then winter followed through its machinations,
crept up and snapped the green head off the year.

A Changed Familiar Tree

On my mind's eye the giant pine that sways,
perfect above the prospect of the years,
is not that other pine which disappears
from nature in two rainy working days,
but one that strives, too steady, too mundane,
against the bluff breeze — a familiar tree
that always sways, in cryptic mimicry
of real change, with a sound like rushing grain —
as if such size, such weight, its age-old powers
against oblivion, could never pass
into pink dust sown on the emerald grass
and damp, turned earth, as small a waste as ours —

II

Our Ancient Sire

For Catherine Tufariello

When I, who led the hunt just yesterday,
began, still bloody, belly full, to tire,
I lay down with my people by the fire,
as in the dark their whispers died away.

How long I searched the flames I couldn't say,
but soon I saw Him there, our ancient Sire
buried when I was beardless, slight, no higher
than tall grass, though my beard has since gone gray.

A child again, afraid to look too long,
I, who am feared, who lead the hunt now, wept
and quailed. His voice, the wind, began to rise.

I knew, then, all that time I'd done Him wrong.
I'd often wondered if in truth He slept
or crept the forests. Now I too am wise.
       And knowing wisdom lies
in dreams and stealth, in what remains unsaid,
I raised a cairn and stained it bloody red,
       that when I, too, am dead,
they—if they overlook my resting-place—
discover, rising from their fires, my face.

A Cellar in Pankow

March 1945

We stay put. From between two hollow halves,
as if it were a Russian doll, our future
egests, each day, a humbler miniature.
We catch ourselves believing this routine.
Spring, summer, fall, and winter: Two each, now,
divide us from our son, six months a Briton.
We share our cordial hosts' good graces, rations,
water, a view, this cellar, consolation.
I have become nearsighted. Isaac, too.
Then, like a picture one might someday enter,
this window, our inevitable view:
automobiles moving blackly through;
the faceless drivers' forward stare; then, closer,
under the ever-damp gray walls of neighbors
invisible to us but often heard,
big, melting sprays of bowed forsythia.
What would one peeking in at us observe?
Stunted life. Life that flows in conduits
of darkened, undiscovered shipwreck hulls.
But maybe also something of himself:
highlight and shadow, thin as his exhalations
dissolving on mid-March, or late November,
or January air. And then one day,
should we continue rising in this way,
madness or death. Forgive the lucky ones
their monumental, necessary crime.
For "it shall not come nigh thee." Or so says
another Jew who fought the Philistines.

The Birthday Gift

She spoke to him all morning in a room
almost as bare and dormant as his mind.
He lurked in his new tank top at the table
she'd bolted down against his sudden thought.
Born wrong that morning thirty years before,
the brain inside his head would always be
as senseless as a fig inside a purse.
His temper was a club. Behind his face
old questions loomed, their answers still forbidden.
He held his shoe as if it were a foot,
and then he flung it, mad at something hidden.
Maybe her son was spared thoughts, as the room
was spared the usual mirror, lamps, and vase.
If he'd had thoughts, he would've flung those too.
She tossed the birthday boy his other shoe.

A Contract

Their love ran out in March; their lease, in June.
He moved where cash allowed, took the room strewn
with near-junk unseen since their wedding day.
Home, then, was like a drawer where one might lock
loose pieces of a fallen antique clock.
She lived in bed, ate oatmeal from a tray,
read comics like a child bored with a cold.
He searched the bars for something nice to hold.

Then, drunk, he'd close his eyes and trace the day,
the day's soft flicker, down to a shrinking dot,
as though a ship were burning, far away.
She saw his razor on the sink, the cot
folded, the room he slept in not at all,
where once she'd wrapped him, waiting, in a shawl,
and, warmed at last, he could pretend to wake.
He waited now, unseen, for no one's sake.

The Abject Bed

She couldn't do a thing, could only stare,
as the white frocks carried her husband out,
up from the abject bed at last. Nowhere
were friends so kind, she heard herself declare
before the costly funeral; though, throughout,
she couldn't do a thing, could only stare.

She mourned her proper year. But then despair
was packed away so she could court self-doubt
as, up from bed at last, she found nowhere
hired one for seeming proper or debonair,
and pay was nil for being the most devout.
She could do nothing! so, she'd sit and stare
at classifieds until her child was there,
driving her to the store.

                    Years went that route,
from bed to store and back at last, nowhere
to go but round and round, no need to wear
more than a robe till life was carried out
and she could do her thing, could finally stare
up from the abject bed, at last nowhere.

Last Moments of Simeon Stylites

Pain shines a little, like a branding scar.
You chose it, yet you gave your flesh the lie,
agnostic of sound sense, which would deny
responsibility for what you are.

You preached no compromise. Yet now you die.
Your spoiled life joins all lives, one frozen star
more in the vain swarm—holiest by far,
yet never more than forty cubits high.

Look there. Across the sand sun draws a bar
of thin shade, where winged shadows seem to fly
over priests, pilgrims, and the shrewd bazaar.

Offer your cheek to the ungiving sky.
Let one eye shut; but keep one eye ajar
and, to the host that hails you, bid good-bye.

The Festival

In the church parking lot, in tents,
the roulette games no one can win
flashed yellow light from painted bulbs
across the lenses of the men.
As it had at the farm or store,
less kept them coming back for more.
From beer, they swayed like corn in rows.
They unfixed stares to wink at wives
whose dead eyes double-crossed their smiles.
Twice each minute, their small hope
spun slowly to a ticking stop,
and crumpled bills were raked away
to God. Then new space at the rope
was cleared for the next bumper crop.

Runaway Daughter

She slept. Sleep was a stupid hiding place.
Rest hadn't come so easily for him.
Running his thumb along her moonlit face,
grown calm, as his had, in the interim,
he wondered what she thought she could escape.
Her head peeped from the quilt beneath her chin
like someone's shoe exposed beneath a drape,
as he rehearsed the ways he might begin.
The ear he chose was downed with light. His chest
throbbed, and the throbbing made him want to pause.
Something suggested it was loveliest
to watch her face a moment how it was.

Introduction to Poetry

For Edgar Bowers

They choose a back road leading from the inn,
the young man and the great and dying man
he's come to see. Over the narrow road
arch oak boughs, crossed amid the partial dark
and bowed with the habitual tact of age.
Consideration for the run-down thing
is what they share, and little else. Rank vines
dangle above the dip and crest of asphalt
on which they walk toward night, seeking the place
where it is understood they must turn back.
This is the only chance, this mustn't fail.
Young man delivers his imperfect part
to old man, who must also hear the sound
of his own shoes on a back road at dusk,
the involuntary interest in the new
cells in his blood carrying his mind past dusk.
But when the young man's voice stops, and their steps'
dry, private sound against the earth alarm
the old man into speech, it is as if
he sat at a clavier, stiffened by age,
and watched his own unpracticed fingers prove
again, unerringly, an ageless passion.
He hears his voice once more, cadence and rest,
weighing, in spite of each step's falling sound
of looking back, how poetry began.

The Story of the Week

Experience was nothing that day. That day was Sunday.

It was impossible to transcend the Western Tradition of Sunday.
But he did not demand a better world.

This he left to the moon, the moon's day, Monday.

Saturday he was maudlin, and may have been in love.
Friday he got phone calls, but wasn't there to answer.

Wherever he was he was not falling in love.

Thursday was bunk. The sack of his heart emptied.
Wednesday was symmetry, a thimbleful of nothing.

What seemed most decisive, redemptive, was Tuesday.
Suffering really meant something to him then.

Monday, last Monday, he felt sure he'd found
the catch in the course of circular motion.

Sunday he did not demand a better world.

Last Chance at Reconciliation

He's certain where he's headed it's too late.
West Broadway glitters in a mist of rain
that amber cones of light elucidate.
He's certain. Where he's headed, it's too late
to stop for flowers, dry off, or get things straight:
a story, his misshapen hat, his brain.
He's certain where he's headed. It's too late.
West Broadway glitters in a mist of rain.

After a Nightmare

The room was hushed. His eyes had dried.
Still, bad thoughts brightened in the dark.
Light faded in, but that light lied.
Each breath was like a grave remark.

His vision warmed as, evil-starred,
he faced his parents' door again,
but this time no one let him in.
His worry made him listen hard.

He nudged the door, then slipped inside
and saw his father's broad, pale back.
The shuddering bed frame seemed to crack
beneath a sound of homicide.

By one o'clock his dad had come
to tuck him in. His mother's face
haunted the doorway like a trace
of phosphor dimming on the thumb.

It was a dream, his father said—
a lie the hush might underscore.
He let the murderer kiss his head,
and then he nodded to the whore.

The Suicide

Water seemed serenely self-justifying.
But it had such elegant urgency, as
all at once she found herself drowning in it,
sure the deepest mysteries must always deepen.

Water squeezed and squeezed with a changeless motion.
Water wasn't easy to finish drinking.
Still, she felt herself to be something rare, some
delicate fern some six miles beneath the surface.

Partial sunlight breaking the ocean's surface
fell in columns, columns that in collapsing
struck her ready eye with a tragic strangeness.

It was hard absorbing herself in dying.
But, at last, she proved to be one absorbed by
columns collapsing.

A Broken Home

The windows fogged. Pots spat. The ham hocks stewed.
Her cleaver knocked through pork and collard greens.
The selfish creature scribbled battle scenes
at the set table, squirming for his food.
Cruel friends had left him in the broken mood
she couldn't mend alone. The lima beans
thawed in the bag. The beets bled. Which cuisines,
she wondered, fed a boy's ingratitude?
She switched the stove off. In his obtuse face
she thought she read past failures paraphrased.
Guilt won, and that day's spoils were cake and milk.
He didn't eat, but sighed—half blame, half grace—
then pitched in, shucking corn. At times, amazed,
she paused to turn a ring that dangled silk.

Schism by Twilight

From where we fought at sunset on the pier,
that huge ungraspable perplexity
of power and motion, light and atmosphere,
could seem to you a token surety,

as if the never-ending blue veneer
and high shell-colored mares' tails we could see
were images to have and to hold dear,
daubed on a jewelry box, but feelingly,

an heirloom of our human family,
but tendered with a smile to us two here:
to brighten all life's rainy subtlety,
console me on my way, and help me bear

my mind, as yours has been borne year by year,
from will to shall, in Cosmic Harmony.

Family Gathering

What love was passed around was like a fruit
perfectly grown and cut to win a prize,
and in the end a fruit, though small, to share
or else be rid of. The grandmother's eyes,
as she bit through the core
to tell her anecdote,
were cryptic and serene, but not yet wise.

The uncle wrestling with an olive jar,
his purple hand striped white, left off to listen.
The grown-up nieces, like two panicked cats,
sat huddled in one corner of the couch.
The father in his chair
brushed back his daughter's hair
and placed the pipe inside the open pouch.

The family came together like a thought
finally uttered once its sense is gone.
The grandma smiled. She spied the eyes she knew
guttering into faces she did not.
The motions of a face
made her confident
and kept her speaking of a distant place,
of ordinary lives remembered slant . . .

Buzzards

. . . She said, "Once, I'd take walks
to the mowed fields at noon.
I'd lie on the dried, blond stalks
and hum my quiet tune
to the mowed fields. At noon,
I'd lie peaceful as death
and hum my quiet tune
under my cooling breath.
I'd lie peaceful, as death
gathered like ashes above me.
Under my cooling breath
I'd ask God, 'Who could love *me*,
gathered from ashes?' Above me
they'd wheel and fall, then rise.
I'd ask God who could love me,
and wait. But they were wise:
They'd wheel and fall, then rise.
I'd lie on the dried blond stalks
and wait. But they were wise,"
she said.
            "Once, I'd take walks . . ."

Alexandra

"A man was distressed in mind because of me. . . . I chose to betake myself alive into the tomb."

For ten years I have known
only this shadow-show
that interrupts the glow
cast on my walls of stone.
I've felt my innocence.
Shifting to bask in it,
I've often found it lit
a darker consequence.

Bright mornings promise spring.
I used to wish for birds,
for music stripped of words.
It comes: fierce, echoing,
strange as the specks of gray
that on the sunlight's dumb,
slow, fluid medium
soar mercifully away.

This evening, stirred by fear,
I looked out at the weather
and spied two forms together.
Did they spy me in here?
Wouldn't they laugh to see
themselves as I must: shades
fading, as twilight fades,
inconsequentially?

My walls are interlaced
with waving shapes, all slight,
all, slowly as the light,
passing like parceled waste.
In the sandy glow
on these walls of stone
I may yet be shown
all I need to know.

A Lot of Noise

Downstairs the diner closed up late again.
The Dumpster lids blew shut below his room.
Before long, he heard barking garbagemen
hurling the trash, the shush-shush of a broom,
the whistle of the last man to depart.
The upstairs dachshund paced, its claws' slow strokes
belaboring the downbeat of his heart.
A television somewhere roared at jokes
he couldn't quite be part of through the brick.
Just once he tumbled fleetingly toward sleep,
but in the fated impact, with a kick,
opened his eyes on darkness two hours deep.
And, in due time, the first pale light of spring
fell on his pillow, soundless, brightening.

Dystopian

The past is fiction,
their will our reason,
and hope an addiction
in that hard season
where our chronic souls'
unalterable goals,
our noblest and best
ideals, deserve us.
People are nervous,
but privately, lest
all that remain
of subclinical pain
be a neat suture.
In our gray future
narcotics are pap
and culture is junk.
Between frozen trunk
and quickening sap,
the civic bargain
is hardly struck.
Hope is furniture.
Survival is luck.
Ethos is jargon.
And once you learn it you're
utterly mastered;
or touched, like Nero,
beautiful bastard,
vestigial person
watching things worsen,
scapegoat and hero.

Retirement

The man became himself again. His health
seemed perfect in the free mornings spent
next to his wife in bed; in afternoons
of reading on the couch and picking which
shoes to wear to restaurants; and in
the night's exquisite weariness, and sleep.

The man became himself again, and after
thirty-two years of selling lithographs,
he thought he had ideas to return to.
His health was proven perfect by the doctor,
a woman, he noticed, twenty years his junior,
and so, to celebrate, he bought an easel.

He thought he had ideas to return to
in the mornings changed to afternoons at the table.
He was healthy during afternoons of staring,
picking shoes to wear the evenings out.
And in the night's exquisite weariness
and sleep, the man became himself again.

The Pig Roast

The afternoon wound down. The pool was calm.
Some children played around the emptied trough.
The small, low town was far enough away
behind the trees to look as though it were
a thread of road, some boxes, a toy steeple
propped on a branch. The parents bustled in
to cocktails when the lightning bugs began.
The children had the country on their shoes.
Outside, they watched the greasy farmhand set
a tractor's broken axle in the half-light.
They trailed him with a hundred aimless questions
until an aunt corralled them in the house.
A wobbly mother volunteered to fight
the crusted shoes and knotted laces off.
Outside, the farmhand closed his day. He crouched
beside the rifle hanging from the fence
and scratched the pig's broad head, then slowly rose
as though he'd left a teacup balanced there.
After the shot, the farmhand turned to spit,
and, with a rag, wiped from his dirty hands
what must have been the day, being done with it,
and turned then to the night, and night's demands.

The Mayor

The light that woke him made him think of town.
It was a pale pink light, shed by a bulb
that droned above the empty road he lived on.
He sat upright in bed,
noticed his posture, how his jutting head
sought equilibrium and not much else.
God was far off. And, like an enemy,
the town was all around.
The sound of the several mills
was nothing but a funeral sob. The hills
were creeping with cattle, the cattle with liver fluke.
His heart was beating this way: stop, stop, stop . . .
God was far off. The town was all around.

Rabbit's Foot

Grandfather rabbit, and grandfather hare,
forgive us, your forgetful progeny,
who unleash dogs to shake you in their jaws,
then sell your hacked-off hands as souvenirs.
Forgive us. Our hearts, too, are very little,
and race with blood as tenuous as our fate:
We also tremble helplessly or flee.
But, with this relic of your ancient luck,
so may we also often procreate,
and burrow always toward the mystery
below, as our grandfather rabbit does.
And may our naked children, as yours do,
grandfather hare, drop always open-eyed
onto the sunlit meadow of despair.

Merrily

"And we sleep all the way; from the womb to the grave we are
never thoroughly awake; but passe on with such dreams, and
imaginations as these ..."

—John Donne

If only their significance were clear.
This quick, green bank. The sun's autistic eye,
oblivious to one more pioneer.
Unmeaning blue, less sky than anti-sky.
West, through the trees' meshed crowns, light scattering
toward such specific ends! Why those? And why
these flexed roots? Why that oak's failed rendering
of coupled elephants in living wood?
Its leaves smell sour, although it feels like spring.
I could go on. *Quis homo?* It's no good:
The more things blur, the clearer I become.
I could go on forever if I could.
Meanwhile, my boat moves downstream, listing some.
The question tails away. Against the prow
pumped gently by the surge, my back goes numb.
Behind, a riot-swept feather or split bough
neither recedes nor gains. As if to steer,
I drop a hand in. Oh, well. Anyhow,
the scenery is mesmerizing here.

Notes

Post Partum: The epigraph is from "The Second Coming," by W. B. Yeats.

War Dims Hopes for Peace: The title is a headline from *Wisconsin State Journal*, December 27, 1965. Lines 1 through 16 are headlines drawn from various news publications between September 11 and September 14, 2001. The typographical error ("Muslins") appeared in the source.

"If Ye Find My Beloved . . .": The title is from Song of Solomon 5:8.

A Changed Familiar Tree: The title is from "Eros Turannos," by E. A. Robinson.

A Cellar in Pankow: The quotation in line 27 is from Psalms 91:7.

Alexandra: Alexandra was a Christian maidservant in fourth-century Egypt. Believing she had seduced a man, she shut herself in a tomb as penance and remained there ten years. The epigraph is from the anchoress's own explanation, as reported in *The Lausiac History of Palladius*. This poem is dedicated to Talia Neffson.

Rabbit's Foot: "[M]ost early European peoples confused the rabbit with the hare, and in time the feet of both animals were prized. . . . The luck attributed to a rabbit's foot stems from a belief rooted in ancient totemism . . . that humankind descended from animals." *Extraordinary Origins of Everyday Things*, by Charles Panati (New York: Harper and Row, 1987).

Merrily: The epigraph and the question in line 10 ("*Quis homo?*") are from John Donne's "Sermon XXVII," which refers to Psalms 89:48: "What man is he that liveth, and shall not see death?"